SAFE & SOUND

A Parent's Guide on Self-Protection for Kids

E. Gordon Franks

Susan Erling

Recommended for Parents with Kids up to age 16

SAFE & SOUND PRODUCTIONS
Copyright ©1990 by E. Gordon Franks
and Susan Erling

SAFE & SOUND PRODUCTIONS
P.O. Box 27174
Golden Valley, MN   55427
612-USA-1234

ISBN

Printed in the United States of America
First Edition

ACKNOWLEDGEMENTS

Consultants: Amber Erling, M. Pat Worley of USA Karate Schools, and Sherokee Ilse of Wintergreen Press

Editor: Ronda Wintheiser

Cover Design: Michael Doyle

Photographers: Carol Ferguson, Gordon Franks, and Diane T. Bush

Graphic Artist: Terry Schultz of H.I.S. Computer Services

Printer: Lakeland Press

Models: Brandon Groth, Dawn Groth, Amber Erling, Jake Erling, Noelle Erling, Dominic A. Forte', Tina Gjerstad, Matthew R. Jogodka, Dave Redding, Kim Redding, Nathan Rogers, Dimitri Santrizos, Paul Santrizos, and Kiersten Stoinski. (All of the models are USA Karate School students or parents.)

Special thanks to Lee Larson of Brooklyn Park, Minnesota for coming to the aid of Amber Erling during her attack.

CONTENTS

THE RIGHT TO SELF-PROTECTION

Our founding fathers strongly believed in our inalienable right to defend ourselves and our families. They also recognized the fact that the government is not designed to protect us at all times. Self-protection is an individual's right and responsibility.

INTRODUCTION

Susan Erling

In September of 1988, I enrolled in karate classes at the USA Karate School in Minneapolis. I was an unlikely black belt candidate: A 35 year-old mother of five children—not your average hard-core athlete. But I joined to get my 12 year-old son in the door. Jake has Cystic Fibrosis and needed this type of body/mind training as a part of his therapy. I planned to leave within a week.

However, it became clear to me almost immediately just how very vulnerable and defenseless I was, meandering through life as if I were immune from violent attack. I was a "perfect victim" and never even knew it. I decided to stay even if Jake left. But it never occurred to me until eight months later that all five of my children should be learning self-defense skills.

In May of 1989, my 14 year-old daughter Amber was the victim of a kidnapping and an attempted rape. It was a shocking, terrible experience. I found it incomprehensible that some demented stranger would randomly choose my daughter, tear her off her bike, steal her, and then try to drag her into the woods to rape her. But how could I know that Amber was in danger? After all, we live in a "safe," suburban neighborhood, she was only a block away from home, and it was still light out. But as I found out later, the odds of being attacked were against Amber. And against your children, too.

Fortunately, Amber did escape because I had taught her some self-defense skills and had instilled in her a self-defensive attitude. **She wasn't a perfect victim.** She fought back; screaming, kicking, punching, clawing, biting, and creating a riotous scene. She didn't weaken, grovel, or succumb to him even though he hurt her and had weapons in the car. The detective on her case later told me that if she hadn't fought back, the attacker might have killed her.

But Amber was able to save her own life with her will to live, her courage, and her self-protection skills. My self-defense training helped to save the life of my first-born child and that is a debt that can never be repaid.

Two days after the attack, Amber and her 11 year-old sister Noelle started karate training. Amber needed to regain some of the physical security which was robbed from her by the attacker. Noelle needed to realize her own power and capabilities. After the attack, she innocently said that she would never have been able to fight back as Amber had because, as she put it, "He might sue me if I hurt him." Needless to say, this attitude astounded and gravely concerned me.

My hope is that this guide will help parents to gain the knowledge to remove themselves and their children from the category of perfect victim. No child should ever be a victim, and certainly, no child should ever be a perfect victim.

Amber and Susan Erling   Photographer: Diane T. Bush

Gordon Franks

When I heard about Amber's attack, I had a sinking feeling in my stomach. I now know that this feeling was the realization that such things really can happen to me or to those close to me!

It's my business to help people handle physically and emotionally threatening situations. To a degree, I have to talk about physical and sexual assault every day in my self-defense and karate classes.

But I still was not prepared for something like this to happen to someone I'm close to. After twenty years of advising people to be aware of potentially dangerous situations and to expect the unexpected, I had been guilty of the same kind of thinking: Bad things happen to other people, not to my family and friends.

Today the family structure is different than it was a generation ago. There are more single parent and two-career families. Subsequently, there seems to be a greater population of "latch key" kids who are on their own many hours in a day without parental supervision. It's more crucial than ever that kids have good self-defense skills since the odds of attack are even higher than in the past. Such skills can give the kids and their parents peace of mind in a time of rising crimes against children. Perhaps they could even save a life.

Fortunately for Amber and her brothers and sisters, their parents had the foresight to prepare their children with a real self-defense skill: KNOWLEDGE. For them and for your children, knowledge can mean confidence...and confidence is your child's most powerful self-defense technique.

My hope is that this book will serve as a crime prevention guide, and help your children to develop a self-protective life-style.

"It's not fair to have to walk around being scared all the time."
-an assaulted child

1

WHY SELF-DEFENSE FOR KIDS?

As parents we want more than anything else for our children to be safe and sound. We want them protected and free from harm. Unfortunately, we live in a violent world where crimes against children are on the upswing; children are being victimized at an alarming rate.

Current crime statistics show that 1 in 4 girls and 1 in 7 boys will be sexually assaulted before the age of 16. Every year the number of physically abused, kidnapped, or murdered children increases. Physical violence against children has become a national tragedy.

Such attacks and acts of violence can range from a shoving match in the school yard to sexual assault to murder. These can be terrifying thoughts to parents. We desperately want to protect our children from harm, but it's not always possible. It's unrealistic to think that you can keep your children safe and sound by keeping them in your "hip pocket," so to speak. Because this is impossible, the kids need for you to teach them how to survive and how to thrive in today's world in the midst of violence. They also need to be given the opportunity to accept responsibility for their own safety.

We cannot allow our children to be the victims of violence just because we have not made them aware of their right to self-protection, their own ability to protect themselves to some degree, and then to give them some real alternatives. We believe it is better to prepare them with a self-defensive attitude, self-defense skills, and self-defense habits. Self-defense training can be the equalizer; some crimes against children can and should be prevented.

Crime prevention experts have stated that learning how to react to a physically threatening situation in spite of fear is what helps children conquer their fear. Just knowing how to yell—a basic technique taught to every new karate student—could be enough to thwart an attack. Screaming may have saved Amber's life.

Knowing how and where to strike an attacker is the next step in preventing your child from becoming another assault, kidnap, or rape statistic. Every time a child yells and resists a bully or an attacker, they help to dispel the myth that children are passive, helpless, perfect victims. No child ever needs to walk around feeling scared all the time.

Will self-defense training turn a normal kid into a mini-Rambo?

For many kids, just the fear of violence is immobilizing. They may cope with their fear by pretending the danger does not exist or by believing naively that "it will never happen to me." Even in their dreams, children as well as adults find themselves paralyzed by terror; unable to react, scream, or escape. And yet dispelling fear and demystifying violence by learning a "violent" art form such as karate may seem an odd solution to the problem! If every child were taught a form of self-defense wouldn't that inadvertently be creating a generation of "mini-Rambos?"

Actually, just the opposite happens. Studies done by Michael E. Trulson, A & M University, and Chong W. Kim and Vernon R. Radgett, Marshall University have shown that children who have developed self-defense skills have "a lower level of anxiety; an increased sense of responsibility; a decrease in the willingness to take risks; they are less likely to be "radical"; they have an increased level of self-esteem; and they are more socially intelligent."

This study also showed that teenagers who have been in trouble at school, with the law, or at home due to their aggressive nature and lack of respect for others, changed dramatically after studying a martial art. According to their parents, they became more respectful and self-disciplined in a very short period of time.

Parents have a responsibility to see that their children have information about people and situations that might cause them harm. And this can be done in an unalarming way. Children must be told about the dangers that exist in our world so that they are able to handle themselves in harmful situations and be able to prevent injury or even save their own lives.

We are not advocating that you scare your kids, but rather that you **enlighten** them. Teach them the difference between healthy fear and fear that borders on paranoia. Knowledge makes children more aware and actually promotes confidence. We believe that confidence is a child's best self-defense tool. When kids are confident and prepared in advance, they can better handle almost any uncomfortable life situation.

But children also need clear and concise information about **how** to remain safe. If they are not taught, their resources will be limited in dangerous situations. Kids who have self-defense training will feel more secure and confident. They won't be immobilized by fear because they know that they have some **real alternatives.** They will still be normal kids, but safer ones.

Can every child learn self-defense?

We believe that every child can learn self-defense or self-protective skills and that they can be taught at a very early age. It begins when mothers and fathers tell their young children, "Don't touch a hot oven," "Don't play in the street," "Don't talk to strangers," "Play close to home," or "Don't accept **anything** from strangers."

By the time they enter kindergarten, kids should know their name, address, telephone number, and where their parents work. They also should be taught how to use a telephone and how to dial 911 for help. By the time they are four years old, they can be taught real safety skills such as kicks, punches, and other self-defense techniques.

Every child can learn some self-defense techniques, including handicapped, tiny, young, or frail children. And both girls and boys can be taught to be equally as powerful and effective.

Can parents teach their children self-defense or do they need to study a martial art?

It's important to know that basic self-defense or self-protective skills are innate; an inborn knowledge, often referred to as "a will to survive." Even newborn babies will cry and attempt to move away from someone or something that is causing them pain or discomfort.

Although such self-protective skills are innate, sometimes they have been tempered and have to be re-learned. Parents and teachers continually remind children not to kick, punch, or yell. They intend to tone down these natural instincts so that the children will more easily conform to society's rules and expectations. This is wise in many situations; however, sometimes there is a good reason for kicking, punching, and yelling: To protect themselves and perhaps even save their own lives.

Parents should teach their children to be **proactive** rather than reactive by teaching them how to recognize dangerous situations and by knowing defense strategies **before** an attack occurs. These lessons do not necessarily need to be taught in a karate school.

So far you have been your child's first and best teacher. You have taught your kids all the basic survival skills; good eating and exercise habits, good grooming and social manners, as well as educating their minds. It's only natural that you would take this nurturing process one step further to include the fundamental skill of self-protection.

However, self-defense classes can help to enhance those natural instincts and refine them through practice. There are definite advantages to getting formal self-defense training in a karate school where your child is taught by an expert. The kids will not only learn how to protect themselves against bullies, but also against adults who might attack them. In a karate school they will learn ways to defend themselves against a person who is twice their size. Your kids can ultimately be trained to be as powerful as a person who weighs 100 pounds more than they do. Also, their self-defense techniques will be more effective because they have been practiced and perfected over time.

Who is a trusted adult?

Who do you want your children to trust and go to for help? Who is a trusted adult?

The Webster dictionary defines "trust" in this way: "To believe in, to place confidence in, to depend upon, to have hope in, or to place in one's care."

A trusted adult is usually someone over 18 years old: A parent, a police officer, a teacher, a neighbor, a coach, or a relative. However, sometimes these people may not be trustworthy. Statistics have shown that many child molesters were once considered "trusted adults" by their victims. **So children must be taught to be initially cautious of everyone.**

Children are by nature very trusting; sometimes too trusting. They need to be taught who to trust, who to listen to, who to follow, as well as who should be allowed to have them in their custody or to touch their bodies.

Just a generation ago kids were instructed by their parents to respect and obey just about all adults. The "bad" people or the "boogie men" were the exceptions to this rule and were easy to pick out. They were the bums, the drunks, and the off-beat characters. Kids were adamantly warned to avoid these people, and to consider everyone else a "trusted adult."

Unfortunately, that's not the case today. It's just too dangerous for children to naively trust every adult. Trust is something that is earned over time, however, it can be lost or forfeited if the trusted person becomes an attacker. We need to help our children to face the reality of the situation in our world today even though it may go against our own upbringing.

"You have to be prepared because you don't expect someone to come running after you."
  -an assaulted child

2

ATTACKS

What is an attack?

An attack is a violent attempt to use force to do harm to another person. Such acts are aimed at injuring or destroying others often by catching them off-guard or unprepared. Types of attacks range from verbal to physical to weaponed with violent attacks being referred to as assaults.

Recognizing that an attack is happening

Often before an attack occurs, the victim somehow feels that something bad is going to happen. Kids are especially intuitive and can often sense that someone or some situation is "weird" or "bad" or "scary" without being told. If your child expresses such thoughts, don't down play them. It's better to encourage your child to avoid that particular person or situation and for you to investigate.

Commonly, survivors of attack recall feeling almost removed from the encounter as if they were observers witnessing the attack rather than being the victims. The mind seems to go "numb" or into "automatic pilot" to deal with the terrifying situation at hand.

On a conscious level the victims know that they are being attacked, but the reality of the situation may be more than the mind can handle. Subsequently, the subconscious mind "protects" the conscious one, making reality seem foggy or out-of-focus, and thus easier to deal with. It may appear to be just a bad, scary dream. But allowing this to happen can be a matter of life and death for a child. **The sooner the child resists; the greater the chances of escape.**

In those first few seconds of the attack, it is crucial that your child's self-defense responses kick in **automatically.** If these responses are learned in advance, they will surface, causing the legs to run, the hands to strike, and yells to roar out of a throat that may be constricted with fear. These life-saving responses will be there **if** they are learned and practiced in advance.

Children can escape dangerous situations and save themselves from harm only if they recognize that they are being attacked and then respond accordingly.

TYPES OF ATTACKS

Verbal Attacks

A verbal attack is an attack on the ego, although it could also be the threat of a physical assault; such as "I'm going to hit you, kill you, etc." A child with a good self-esteem can walk away from a verbal attack such as name-calling without feeling like a failure, feeling shame, or losing self-esteem. A child with poor self-esteem feels the need to retaliate, even against something so minor as name-calling.

Most attacks by other children will be verbal ones and they can be effectively dealt with by ignoring the verbal attacker, walking away, or asking a trusted adult for help. However, some verbal attacks do lead to physical ones.

This is an example of how a child might react to a verbal attack from another child: A bully calls the kid a "wimp". The kid turns to walk away, but the bully moves towards him. The kid turns, raises his palm, and assertively says, "Leave me alone," then turns around and starts to walk away again. Then the bully runs up and shoves him from behind. The kid straightens up, turns sideways, and repeats, "Leave me alone," but gets shoved from the front. The situation has turned from a verbal to a physical attack in a matter of seconds.

Physical Attacks

A physical attack is an attack on the body. Kids can be taught to know when a physical attack is likely to happen, such as when they are "cornered," out-sized, outnumbered, or if they are hit first and/or repeatedly. The child will then be forced to make his or her own judgement call in these situations, knowing that physical defense measures should only be used as a last resort. **Yelling and running away to get help should always be the first response.**

Physical attacks can range from pulling hair, shoving, and punching confrontations to rape, kidnapping, and murder. Obviously, the range of physical assault is widely varied, so your child's self-defense responses should fit the situation. With education your child can learn which response is the most appropriate and effective one.

It's important that parents encourage their kids to discuss their experiences with bullies and shouldn't dismiss the incidents as just "kid stuff." **Physical violence is not acceptable behavior from anyone.** It's better to give your kids alternatives to handling the situation, explaining what may or may not be appropriate responses. Then you have to give them **your permission** to use self-defense techniques if necessary.

Moreover, parents need to be aware that both they and their child should be prepared to accept the consequences of the judgement call. For instance, your child's school may have a rule that anyone caught fighting on the school grounds will automatically get detention or suspension. You, as a parent, need to decide whether it's more important for your child to put up with continued beatings or harassment from a bully or to fight back and stop the attacks and then accept the punishment. You must support your child's decision even if it isn't what you would have chosen. However, if the self-defense technique used in your opinion was not an appropriate one, you should go over other options and do some re-educating.

Weaponed Attacks

In our opinion, there are little or no **direct defense measures** that children should take when attacked with a weapon such as a gun, a knife, or a club. Weapons can maim or kill a child in a matter of seconds. It should be assumed that the attacker most likely will not hesitate to use the weapon if a victim needs to be subdued or controlled.

Although martial arts schools may teach a kid how to directly defend against a particular weapon, we feel that it's wiser and safer for a child **not** to directly resist at all. Instead, a child should resist in an indirect way by looking for an opportunity to escape when the attacker is distracted or slightly off-guard. And again, the means of escape is **yelling and running for safety**.

Instruct your child to do whatever the attacker says under these extreme circumstances. Nothing is worth risking mutilation or death. Nothing. With proper care victims can recover emotionally and physically from violent attacks...if they live. Preserving life is the single most important motivation during a weaponed attack.

However, when explaining such attacks to your children, it's crucial that you explain the difference between television and movie weaponed attacks and real-life ones. There is no comparison between the two; one is fiction, the other is harsh reality. None of us are G.I. Joes or Rambos who can escape unharmed from bullets, knives, or clubs. Unfortunately, such stunts have been portrayed in an appealing way to our children, making them want to emulate these fictitious heros. But that hero-worship must be dispelled in order for a child to see the incredible danger of weaponed attacks.

"I can't look at people now without wondering what they can do to me or how I can defend myself."
   -an assaulted child

3

SELF-DEFENSE TOOLS

Our children are not as defenseless as they may seem. Each child already has some valuable self-defense tools and other skills can be developed over time. Some of these tools are: Self-confidence, a clear mind, a strong will, adrenaline, assertiveness, body language, and a self-protective attitude.

Self-Confidence

Self-confidence is a conviction of one's own self-worth, a general optimism concerning one's own accomplishments and capacities, and a certainty of succeeding at whatever is attempted. It's believed that children who are self-confident will be able to achieve more, express themselves better, and command a certain respect from others.

Self-confidence is instilled in children through love, praise, encouragement, guidance, and knowledge. Achieving success in their life endeavors enhances their self-confidence or self-esteem, making them want to aspire even higher. Confidence is reflected in how a person walks and talks; in nearly every outward physical act.

Self-confident kids are easy to spot. They are poised, self-assured, and secure without being arrogant or bullies themselves. They are not the type of children who are likely to be picked on by bullies or chosen as easy targets by assailants. Self-confidence is a powerful weapon and the greatest self-defense tool.

Parents need to help their children to establish and maintain a positive self-image so that they can better deal with other children and adults. Encourage them to have a general optimism about life, to speak in a direct, confident way, to walk with the chin held high and the shoulders back, to make eye contact with people, and to respond to questions decisively. However, if you are uncertain as to how to promote confidence in your child, seek professional advice.

A Clear Mind

Keeping a clear mind and using one's wits is crucial for a child during an attack. This will help enable your child to think, make choices, and react in spite of fear. A clear mind will enable your children to make good decisions under stressful circumstances.

Panicking is the opposite of keeping your wits about you. Sudden, over-powering fear can make even the strongest child become confused and simply panic. Panicking can be just as lethal as not attempting to resist, escape, or protect yourself.

When a child panics, the mind goes blank or becomes jumbled and all sensible thought seems to vanish. Thus, the child becomes a far easier and more of a perfect victim. Knowledge helps to prevent panic. When the mind and the body have been trained to react in a self-protective way, they do so reflexively. Subsequently, your child will be less likely to panic or become paralyzed by fear.

A Strong Will

Every parent knows the "power" of willful children. Their desire or determination towards a particular end can surpass the patience or the will of the parent. A child in pursuit of a gooey cookie in a cookie jar atop a six-foot refrigerator concentrates on his or her mission without regard for reason or consequence. The will is so focused that the child can move a heavy chair, scale a counter top, and climb the side of a slippery refrigerator to get to the prize.

As children mature their willfulness is often tempered by their parents and the school system so that they can more easily adapt to society's rules and expectations of them when they grow up. Sometimes, this tempering results in an unmotivated child.

However, self-defense training can help to re-train the will, recapturing some of the lost determination or motivation by creating new reasons to use the dormant will; such as resisting a bully or an adult attacker. Where there's a will...

A strong will is a powerful self-defense tool. It can prevent someone else from imposing **their** will on your child. This emotional strength can help to enhance physical strength when needed and parents should try to resist the temptation to change a child who is too willful. That willfulness can be transformed into a resolute determination that may be the deciding factor as to whether or not your child remains safe and sound in the future.

Adrenaline

"Fight or flight" is a natural bodily response to being startled, frightened, or shocked. This happens when a person experiences extreme emotional distress or when something alarming suddenly happens. Remember how it feels when someone sneaks up and leaps out at you and yells "Boo!"? You jump, your heart races, and you may even break out in a cold sweat. These common reactions are the result of a sudden release of natural adrenaline in your system.

Adrenaline is a hormone secreted in the body by small, ductless glands called the adrenals. It causes a faster heartbeat and an increase of sugar in the blood. This sudden rush of adrenaline makes us instinctively do one of two things: Run away or stay and fight. This "fight or flight" response is automatic and using this "rush" constructively can be a secret weapon in self-defense. It can make a child's legs run faster, a fist punch harder, and create unknown strength in even the smallest body. Adrenaline is another valuable self-defense tool.

Making your children aware of this physical response is another piece of information which will help them to develop better self-protection skills. With proper training, they can learn how to make a quick estimation of a potentially dangerous situation and then make an appropriate and instantaneous judgement call whether to run or to fight.

We believe that the best first response is always to flee or to run away when possible. However, sometimes the need to stay and fight is in order and necessary, but should only be done as a **last resort**.

Children who have self-defense training can learn through practice how to make good, quick judgments about whether to fight or flee. They can also learn to use their adrenaline rush in a positive way if we teach them how.

Assertiveness

There is a definite difference between being assertive and being aggressive. People who are assertive are disposed to bold or confident behavior. Aggressive people often behave in a manner that is forceful, especially intended to dominate, master, or control another person.

Sometimes people confuse assertiveness with aggressiveness and even think that self-defense training will turn their normal kid into an aggressive, hostile child. However, quite the opposite actually happens. Scientific evidence supports the hypothesis that martial arts training results in a **decrease** rather than an increase in aggressiveness, according to a study done by T.A. Nosanchuk of Carleton University.

An assertive child speaks with definite conviction, leaving no doubt as to his or her feelings or intentions. An aggressive child speaks in a belligerent, unprovoked way, often times using foul language or character slurs. Verbal assertiveness often **prevents** a physical attack while verbal aggression tends to lead to physical violence.

Assertiveness is yet another important self-defense tool and should be developed and practiced.

During a verbal confrontation, assertive responses might be: "Leave me alone," "Go away," "No, you're not," "I'm not going with you," or "Stay away from me." Assertive phrases along with assertive body language, such as direct eye contact, an erect posture, and a commanding voice, will often make a bully or an adult attacker turn and leave. They can be intimidated by a powerful, yet non-violent show of strength. Remember that these people want easy victims that they can overpower quickly.

When a child can say, "Leave me alone," and mean it, the bullies or attackers will sense the conviction behind the words and will look for less assertive victims.

Body Language

Body language is an interesting self-defense tool. As the old cliche' goes, "Actions speak louder than words."

Without actually using any self-defense techniques, your children's body language can "speak" for itself and relay their thoughts and feelings in a forceful way. Body language tells a story about your child and may prevent an attack from ever happening.

Some self-protective body language includes: Making direct eye contact with the attacker, being alert and watchful, using an authoritative voice that is level and direct, keeping erect and proper body stances with the shoulders back and the chin held high, having stern or serious facial expressions, using hand gestures, such as the palm out which indicates a stopping motion, and using a medium stride instead of small, quick steps.

Sometimes it might be important to **use** assertive body language even when one does not **feel** assertive. It's possible to become an **actor** for the moment and fool the attacker. After all, courage is not the absence of fear; it is the willingness to act in spite of fear.

A Self-Protective Attitude

An attitude is a certain frame of mind or a way of looking at the world around us. As parents, we encourage our children to view life in an optimistic way or to have a positive attitude. But do we also encourage our children to have a self-protective attitude?

Having a self-protective attitude in a world where just being a kid is a risky business is a crucial self-defense tool. This tool is another way to beat the staggering odds against your children.

A self-protective attitude reinforces the idea that every child is entitled to be safe from harm; that no child deserves to be attacked; and that no child ever needs to be a "sitting duck" or a passive, easy, perfect victim.

Each and every child has the right to self-protection and it begins in the mind, in the heart, and in the attitude. It also begins when parents make their children aware of their rights and promote such life-saving attitudes.

Safe & Sound

"Now if I were to be attacked again, I could really get him!"
-an assaulted child

4

SELF-DEFENSE TECHNIQUES

Children cannot control the violence in the world around them, but they can learn to control their own actions.

Self-defense techniques do not necessarily consist of sensational or daredevil moves, but of **whatever works** in dangerous situations. A sharp poke in the eyes by a five-year-old could be just as effective as a 360 degree round kick executed by a martial artist. If it stops an attack—it was successful.

Ineffective responses like panicking, helplessly screaming with the eyes closed, or pounding on the chest of an attacker (which is the strongest part of the body) can be unlearned.

Every child can learn to do some simple self-defense techniques. These skills can be a way to stop a bully from harassing and hurting your child as well as to prevent a more serious assault. Although it is usually not necessary nor recommended that kids use harsh techniques when dealing with other children, we believe that when a child must defend him or herself against an adult attacker, **no technique is too harsh**.

Each body is made up of a collection of "lethal weapons" and "vulnerable targets." The weapons are feet, hands, elbows, knees, teeth, voice, legs, and the whole body. The targets are eyes, solar plexus (or stomach), groin, shin, instep, ears, nose, knees, and throat. Combining a weapon with a target is what self-defense techniques are all about. The following pages will show various techniques which you can practice with your child.

To gain the maximum benefits from formal self-defense training, most karate instructors recommend that a student take classes 2-3 times per week. However, when teaching your child at home, realize that you are teaching a **self-protective lifestyle** rather than a particular technique.

You will need to decide for yourself just how often you will need to instruct and discuss self-defense skills and attitudes with your children. Do know that the more they hear it; the more likely it will be retained. Kids under age 16 are forgetful and the ideas and attitudes will need to be reinforced over time. Once usually is not enough. However, also know that sometimes a child only needs to hear an idea once and it will resurface when and if the need arises.

WEAPON: THE VOICE

Effective voice uses like yelling, shouting, screaming, or using assertive language should not be underestimated. The majority of attacks can be stopped by using the voice to startle or intimidate the attacker or to attract attention from others who might offer help.

TECHNIQUES: Loud and continuous yelling or shouting words like, "Help!" "Stop!" "Rape!" "Fire!" or "No!" Screaming or making a long, shrill, piercing sound or a cry. In a level or direct voice, use assertive phrases like, "Leave me alone," "Stay away from me," or "No, I won't go with you."

TARGET: The ears of the attacker and any potential rescuers.

AGE OF THE CHILD: Any child.

TYPE OF ATTACKER: Voice techniques are effective on both bullies and adults.

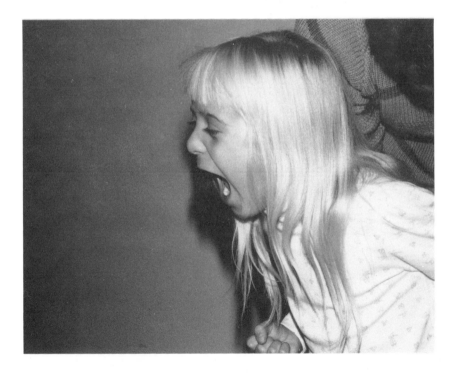

WEAPON: THE LEGS

Along with yelling, the first and best self-defense technique is walking or running away from the attacker. Running away from a potentially dangerous situation should not be viewed as cowardly, but rather as wise and self-protective.

TECHNIQUES: Walk away in swift, rapid steps, run, or use a bike.

TARGET OR INTENT: To escape from the situation by removing yourself from the immediate area and seeking help from a trusted adult.

AGE OF THE CHILD: Any child can walk or run away, however, older children may have a greater chance of escaping because they can move faster.

TYPE OF ATTACKER: Works well on both bullies and adult attackers.

Safe & Sound

WEAPON: THE FEET

The feet are mainly used in self-defense situations to kick or stomp on a vulnerable body part of an attacker with the intent to cause injury and facilitate your child's escape.

TECHNIQUES: Hold the ankle tight and strike forcefully with the foot. A kick to the stomach can take an attacker's air, one to the throat can crush a windpipe, and one to the nose can break it.

TARGETS: The instep, shin, knees, groin, stomach, ribs, throat, face, especially the eyes and the nose.

AGE OF THE CHILD: Ages 4-8 years should aim for the instep, shin, knee, and the groin. Ages 9-12 years should aim for the instep, shin, knee, groin, and the stomach. Ages 13-16 years should aim for the instep, shin, knee, groin, stomach, throat, or face.

TYPE OF ATTACKER: On bullies, kick to the stomach. On adult attackers, kick at all targets. NO HOLDS BARRED ON ADULT ATTACKERS!

WEAPON: THE HANDS

The hands can be used to shove, punch, stab, slap, grab, squeeze, pull, or box the ears. Hand techniques combined with foot techniques can hurt an attacker enough to make an escape possible.

TECHNIQUES: Shove with both hands, punch with the fist in a sharp, swift blow, stab with the fingertips to penetrate or pierce, grab and squeeze tightly such as to the groin, slap with the palm, strike with the heel of the palm, pull the hair, or box the ears with both hands cupped.

TARGETS: Eyes, ears, hair, groin, stomach, throat.

AGE OF THE CHILD: Ages 4-8 years can stab the eyes and box the ears if they are picked up or they can punch to the groin if they are on the ground. Ages 9-12 years can punch to the groin or the stomach. Ages 13-16 years can punch or grab and squeeze the groin, punch to the stomach, or strike to the throat.

TYPE OF ATTACKER: On bullies, punch, shove, slap, or pull the hair. On adult attackers, use every and all techniques. NO HOLDS BARRED ON ADULT ATTACKERS!

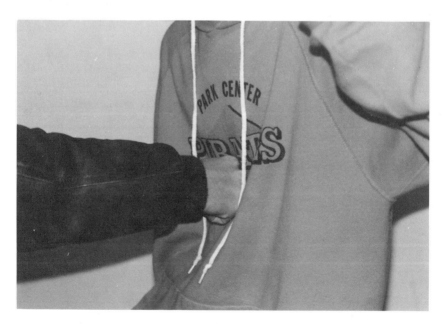

Safe & Sound

WEAPON: THE ELBOWS

A bent elbow is hard and sharp and can be a powerful weapon when jabbed into a vulnerable area.

TECHNIQUES: Jabbing, poking, or thrusting the elbow sharply and rapidly. An elbow to the groin can incapacitate a male attacker quickly; to the stomach can take the air; and to the face can break a nose.

TARGETS: Groin, stomach, throat, face, spine.

AGE OF THE CHILD: Ages 4-8 years can elbow to the groin. Ages 9-12 years can elbow to the groin and the stomach. Ages 13-16 years can elbow to the groin, stomach, throat, face, or spine.

TYPE OF ATTACKER: On bullies, elbow to the stomach. On adult attackers, elbow all targets. NO HOLDS BARRED ON ADULT ATTACKERS!

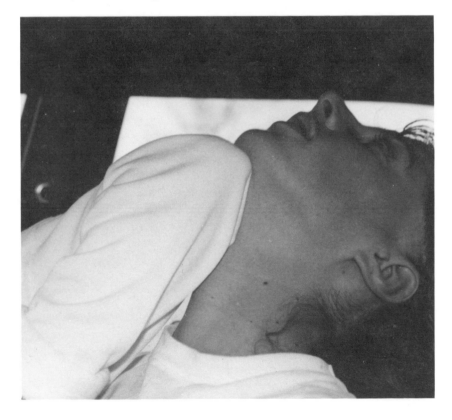

WEAPON: THE KNEES

When bent tightly, the knees can be a devastating weapon, especially when driven with a lot of body force.

TECHNIQUES: Ramming, driving, or thrusting the knee into vulnerable areas to crush or otherwise injure.

TARGETS: Groin, stomach, face.

AGE OF THE CHILD: Ages 4-8 years may be tall enough to knee an attacker in the groin. Ages 9-12 years can knee to the groin or stomach. Ages 13-16 can knee to the groin, stomach, or the face if the attacker is leaning forward.

TYPE OF ATTACKER: On bullies, knee to the stomach. On adult attackers, knee anywhere. NO HOLDS BARRED ON ADULT ATTACKERS!

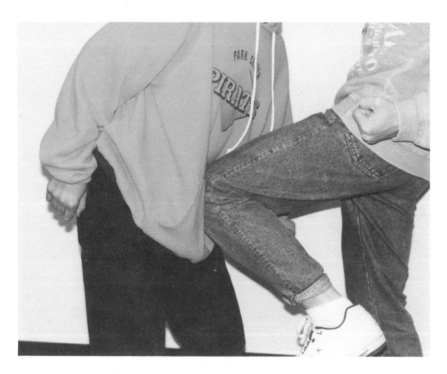

WEAPON: THE WHOLE BODY

Using the whole body can be effective, especially when combined with other techniques. The intent is to move around to break free of the hold.

TECHNIQUES: Squirming, bending or twisting the body, wiggling or moving quickly and irregularly from side to side or struggling forcefully.

TARGETS OR INTENT: Break an arm hold.

AGE OF THE CHILD: All ages can squirm or wiggle or struggle about if they are picked up in the attacker's arms or grabbed and held with both arms.

TYPE OF ATTACKER: Usually bullies won't try to pick up another child. On adult attackers, use all body techniques. NO HOLDS BARRED ON ADULT ATTACKERS!

WEAPON: THE TEETH

Biting may not seem like a legitimate way to defend oneself. However, if biting can prevent injury to your child or facilitate an escape it should be done.

TECHNIQUES: Using the teeth to bite, seize, tear, puncture, or otherwise wound the skin of an attacker. A bite can often be used to "buy time" or to create an opening for escape or the use of other techniques.

TARGETS: The nose, ears, cheeks, lips, or any other part of an attacker's body.

AGE OF THE CHILD: Any age child can bite effectively.

TYPE OF ATTACKER: Use the teeth on both bullies and adult attackers.

"I used to think that people were all good and sweet and that bad stuff just happened on the news. But it happened to me..."
    -an assaulted child

5

ATTACKERS

Who might attack your child?

Many attackers may not look dangerous, mentally deranged, or appear to be on drugs. They are not necessarily brown- or black-skinned people, nor are they exclusively male. However, they are usually insecure or desperate people who are uncertain of themselves and their own motives. Often they attempt to prey upon and hurt children in order to bolster their own sagging self-esteem.

These attackers can often be intimidated by a show of confidence, strength, or will and they are not looking for equal opponents. They want easy targets; weak and helpless victims that won't fight back. Contrary to popular belief, passive, submissive behavior will **increase** the chance that the attack will be completed—whether it's a punching match, rape, kidnapping, or a murder attempt. **Children must be taught effective resistance methods to use against any and all attackers.**

Some of the people who might possibly attack or hurt your child are other children (bullies), strangers, acquaintances, friends, and relatives.

TYPES OF ATTACKERS

Other Children (Bullies)

Your children's primary concerns or fears will probably be with other children who might be calling them names or pushing them around. We call these young intimidators "bullies." Sometimes a group of bullies will even band together to "rule" a particular play area.

To a kid, being bullied can feel terrible. From a child's perspective, it may feel like it's a life and death situation. Most of these bully attacks are verbal, however, some are physical ones.

Why do kids bully? It's believed that kids bully other kids due to low self-esteem. They are aggressive and have a need to control, dominate, or belittle others to bolster their low self-images. Both boys and girls bully. Their physical attacks are not necessarily provoked, but probably follow a series of verbal attacks. Sometimes they are acting out family violence; they may be victims themselves and are striking out at others as a symptom of their own pain.

Effective Resistance

Kids need to be prepared for this kind of violence or intimidation because chances are that it will happen to them if it hasn't happened already. Go over the alternatives and give your kids options for handling bullies. Some options might be: Telling a teacher, walking away, giving the bully what he or she wants, running home or for help, calling out for help, or staying and physically defending themselves.

However, be sure to stress to your children that the use of self-defense measures should always be done as a last resort. Physical defense techniques should never be in any way associated with aggressive physical violence. Instead, the use of assertive phrases and assertive body language is strongly recommended when dealing with bullies.

Try to encourage your children to tell you everything, especially if they are being picked on, robbed, extorted from, or abused by anyone. It's so important for you to report all such incidents to the school authorities, to the appropriate parents, or to the police to hopefully, prevent future attacks.

BULLY PUNCHES GIRL IN THE STOMACH

Bully punches girl in the stomach

Girl turns sideways and says, "Stop it. Leave me alone!"—but the bully attempts to punch her again.

Girls blocks the punch, then knees the bully to the body.

Bully goes down and the girl runs for safety.

BULLY PUNCHES BOY IN THE FACE

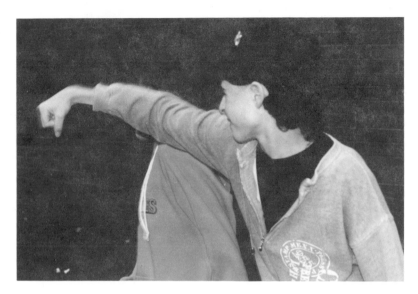

Bully punches boy in the face.

Boy steps back, turns sideways, puts his palm out, and says, "Quit it. Go away!"—but the bully attempts another punch.

Kid protects himself from the next punch and then kicks the bully to the body.

Bully goes down and boy runs for safety.

Strangers

Parents worry about their children's safety and usually advise them not to talk to strangers. But can a child tell the difference between a stranger that might attack them and a trustworthy adult? Sometimes it's hard to tell.

The concept of "stranger" may be hard for a child to understand. It's confusing when "safe" strangers look dangerous and "dangerous" strangers look safe. How can your child determine which strangers may be potential threats and which can be trusted in case of an emergency?

We believe that the only solution is to teach your children to be initially cautious of everyone. However, to prevent an unhealthy paranoia, it's important for you to also help your children to understand that many strangers are helpful and kind while making them aware that there are those who are dangerous. Since it's not always easy or possible to tell the good from the bad, **children must be taught to be initially cautious of everyone.**

Child attackers have many different and inventive ways to lure kids into dangerous situations. It's crucial to make your children aware of such lures, which may appear innocent, but aren't.

According to Kenneth Wooden in his booklet, *A Guide To Prevent Abduction*, child abductors have common lures which include: Posing as an authority figure, bribing, offering fame, love, or an appealing job, asking for assistance, making threats, or using an emergency or a fun situation to their advantage.

Effective Resistance

Due to the size difference, a child cannot physically over-power an adult attacker. Instead, they must learn to use immediate and effective defensive techniques with the intent to do serious damage. In the case of resisting an adult attacker, we believe that **no holds should be barred.**

STRANGER GRABS GIRL FROM BEHIND

Stranger grabs girl from behind.

Girl yells "Help! Help me!" and bites the attacker's arm.

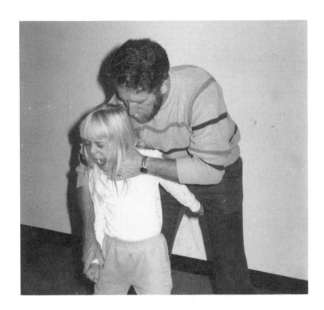

Girl continues to yell and strikes to the attacker's groin with her fist. He loosens his hold on her.

Girl yells and runs for safety.

STRANGER GRABS BOY BY THE WRIST

Stranger grabs boy by the wrist.

The boy yells "No! Help!", grabs his own fist, pulls his hand away, and stomps on the attacker's knee.

Safe & Sound

The attacker picks up the boy and the boy yells and wiggles his body around, which loosens his grip.

The attacker drops the boy and the boy runs for safety.

Acquaintances

By the time your children enter junior high school around the age of twelve, they begin to spend more and more time away from home. Their circle of friends widens and the opportunity to do more social activities increases. Their ties with parents and home tend to loosen as they begin to explore the world a little more and try to find their place in it.

As parents, you will find that it is no longer easy nor always possible to know all of your children's friends like you did when they were younger. You also may not have as much influence on who they choose to befriend. As a result, your children may inadvertently put themselves in situations that might be harmful or unsafe without even realizing it. This is especially true of teenage girls.

Unfortunately, it's commonplace today for a girl to accept a date from a boy or a man that she has recently met and doesn't know very well. (Accepting dates only with people a girl knows well would be a wise self-defensive choice.) She may expect the date to consist of a movie and a pizza, and is stunned and unprepared to deal with a young man who intends to have sex with her...with or without her permission. This is referred to as "date rape."

Some boys or men, especially when under the influence of drugs or alcohol, may become sexually aggressive or abusive to a young girl. They may expect sex as a "reward" for paying for the date. Even if the girl verbally resists, it often isn't enough to stop the attack. Sometimes, it takes more.

Effective Resistance

If a young woman is in a situation where she has said "no" to a sexually aggressive date, and he does not stop, she should use self-defense techniques to facilitate an escape. For example, if she is pinned against a car door, she can stab to the eyes of the attacker or strike with her fist to the groin. Then she must run for help if the date is not willing at this point to take her home or to safety.

So called "date rape" is illegal and sometimes preventable. It's wise to advise your daughter to double-date or group-date until she knows the boy or the man better and to avoid situations in which she is isolated from other people. This should give you and her a little more peace of mind.

BOY ATTACKS GIRL ON A DATE

Boy sexually attacks girl in a car.

She yells "No! Rape!" and when he doesn't stop, she elbows him to the face.

She continues to struggle with him, then strikes to the groin with her fist.

He releases her and she gets out of the car and runs for safety.

Friends and Relatives

Statistics show that in 75% of sexual assault cases, the victim knows the assailant, even if it's only on a first-name basis. It's unsettling to think that people can hurt a child whom they know and love.

Kids can be attacked or harmed by friends of the family. Often children are sexually attacked by family friends, perhaps during a party at the child's home. Babysitters, coaches, neighbors, and friends of older siblings may also attack a child, so again, children need to always be aware and cautious of everyone to a degree.

Kids can also be attacked and hurt by relatives. We realize that this may be an unthinkable thought, but it's a very real problem that we feel needs to be addressed even though we are uncomfortable with the idea, too.

Child abuse is a terrible type of attack. The abuse may be verbal, physical, emotional and/or sexual. Child abuse evokes a vehement response in the majority of people because it seems like it is the least likely type of violence to occur. However, the incidence of reported child abuse has doubled in the past decade. It's a horrendous family problem where every member is a victim and the abused children often victimize other kids and even their own children later in life.

Many times the children are not even sure that they are being attacked or abused. They may think that this particular behavior is normal. But it's not. It's disgraceful and demeaning.

The abusive parents are often untrusting people who may be using alcohol or drugs. They may have been abused children themselves or may be isolated or separated from family and friends. Often times the family does not get help until the suspected abuse is reported by someone, like a teacher or a neighbor, to the authorities, the child is severely injured, or killed.

Parental kidnapping is another type of crime against children which is increasing today. 100,000–400,000 American kids are victims of parental kidnapping each year. It's important to know that it is **illegal** for a non-custodial parent to take a child from the custodial one; all states have laws that prohibit this action.

Abducting your own child usually is not an act of love, but an act of anger and/or revenge. Often it is not in the best interest of the abducted child. These children may not be safe with the kidnapping parent; many becoming victims of physical or sexual abuse within a year. Parents that kidnap their own children have been shown to be emotionally unstable with histories of violence and abuse.

It's imperative for a child to know who is the custodial parent and **who is not** in order to possibly prevent such an abduction. 20-30% of abducted children are never seen by the custodial parent again.

Effective Resistance

Are we advocating that children be taught to fight back against a mother, a father, an uncle, or a neighbor? In a sense, "yes." They can fight back by recognizing that they are victims, and then by telling a trusted adult, running for help, calling 911 and as a last resort, using self-defense techniques. Once the conspiracy of silence is broken, the family can get help and hopefully, the child's life can be saved.

GIRL IS SEXUALLY ATTACKED BY A FAMILY FRIEND

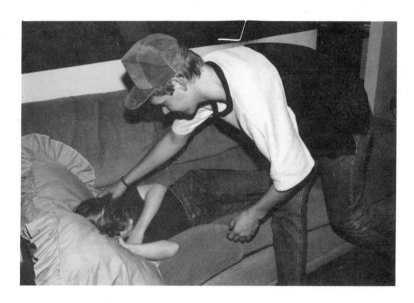

Girl is sexually attacked while lying down.

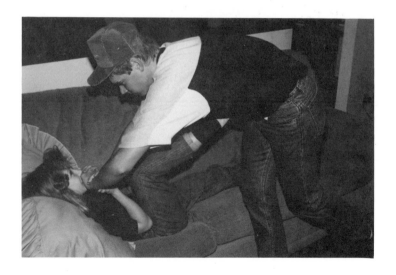

She yells "Help! Rape!" and knees him to the body.

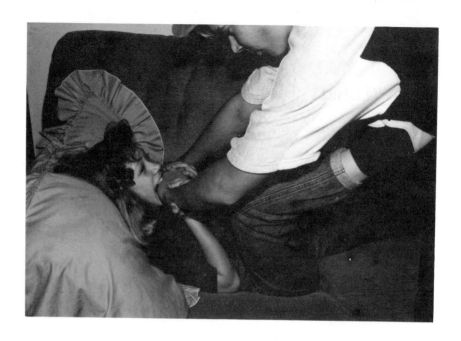

Girl bites the hand that is clamped over her mouth and pushes the man off her.

While he's down, the girls yells loudly and runs for safety.

Safe & Sound

A NON-CUSTODIAL PARENT ATTEMPTS TO KIDNAP HER OWN CHILD

A non-custodial parent picks up her child.

Child yells "No! Help! Put me down!" and then boxes the parent's ears.

The parent drops the child.

The child yells and runs for safety.

"Karate has given me an attitude that I don't have to be the perfect little victim that I may appear to be."
    -an assaulted child

6

ROLE-PLAYING UNSAFE SITUATIONS

We suggest that you role-play possibly unsafe or potentially threatening situations with your children. The intent is not to frighten them, but to help them develop a healthy awareness, and to think through their alternatives. With your help, your children can develop safety skills, attitudes, and habits; a self-protective lifestyle. Hopefully, when kids have these skills the number of child victims will lessen.

Begin role-playing by asking your children the following questions and then wait for their responses. Talk about their reactions, pointing out whether they would be effective or ineffective resistance. Would the action stop an attack? Could the technique create a means of escape? Always remember that yelling and running away should be the first response; staying and using self-defense techniques are a last resort.

- What would you do if a bully shoved you off the steps of a school bus?
- What would you do if a bully hit you with a stick?
- What would you do if a bully punched you in the stomach?
- What would you do if a stranger tried to pull you into his or her car?
- What would you do if a stranger tried to pick you up and take you away?
- What would you do if an adult, who wasn't supposed to, tried to touch you on "private" parts of your body?
- What would you do if your date tried to force you to have sex?

"I wish every child knew what I do now about protecting myself."
-an assaulted child

7

SELF-DEFENSE HINTS AND HABITS

Thinking and reacting in a self-defensive way needs to become a habit or a way of life for your child. These types of behavior patterns will eventually become automatic **if** they are taught and practiced. Good habits are a precious commodity and having good self-defense habits can be critical to keeping your children safe and sound in the future. Below is a list of safety hints that can become safety habits in time.

Safety Hints

- Never bike or play any where alone; travel in pairs.
- Call 911 if you need the help of the police.
- Always keep a quarter with you in case you ever need to make an emergency call for help. Calling "0" for the operator or 911 are free calls from a pay telephone.
- Ask a trusted adult before accepting anything from a stranger.
- Ask a trusted adult before entering the house or the car of a stranger or before following a stranger on foot. Never hitchhike!
- Know where a trusted adult can be reached at all times.
- Be sure a trusted adult knows where you are at all times. Develop a routine of notifying this person by telephone every time you change locations.
- Stay away from unlit, isolated, or unfamiliar streets or alleyways; use heavily traveled roads instead.

- Tell a trusted adult if you have encountered a person who acts in a scary or an unusual way.
- Do not give out information over the telephone to strangers, such as your name, address, or the whereabouts of your parents.
- Do not let anyone into the house without the permission of a trusted adult.
- Do not go near a stranger who may be calling out to you.
- Tell a trusted adult if you are ever touched inappropriately, such as on "private" parts of your body (the bathing suit area).
- Use play areas that are city approved where the police are readily available.
- Don't wear clothing with your name on it because it is a way for an attacker to familiarize him or herself with you.
- Immediately tell a trusted adult if you are attacked.
- Don't take safety for granted even if you are fit or fast or know self-defense techniques.
- Carry a whistle to blow in case of an attack.

As with all important lessons, repetition is the key to retention. You will need to repeat these safety hints again and again to your children until they are remembered and practiced.

During the process of writing this book, Susan sat down with her seven-year-old twins, Luke and Rachael, and discussed all of the safety hints previously listed. She explained the purpose of each hint and answered their questions, making sure that they understood the ideas that she was trying to relay. Afterwards, she felt that they did understand the material until the next day when they went to tell their older siblings about their new-found knowledge.

True, the majority of the hints were surprisingly accurate, "...don't play alone...call 911 for help...don't go near strangers..." However, when they got to the one about telling a trusted adult if they were ever touched on their "private" parts or the bathing suit area, the message somehow got jumbled.

In all seriousness, Rachael told her sisters and brother never to let anyone touch you in a **business suit**! Needless to say, all of the safety hints were repeated, again and again, until they were fully understood.

"By the time I saw him running towards me to help, I was already kissing myself goodbye."
-an assaulted child

8

IN DEFENSE OF OTHER CHILDREN

As your children's self-defense skills become more refined, they will become more aware of impending danger, not only for themselves, but for other children. They will begin to realize that **everyone** has the right to self-protection and recognize their unique responsibility to come to the aid of others. Helping others is an old-fashioned value which, unfortunately, is not widely practiced today.

But to what length should a child go to protect another child? There are many things that kids can do, but most importantly, **they must do something!** Intervention can be life-saving.

If your child sees two other kids involved in a physical confrontation, he or she should try to break up the fight by yelling "Stop!" or "Help!" and then by running to get help from a trusted adult or the police.

If your child witnesses a weaponless adult attacking another a child, it's important that the witnessing child move toward the incident, making his or her presence known by yelling and shouting. This commotion will in many cases stop an attack.

However, if you child witnesses a **weaponed** attack, he or she should run to the nearest telephone and dial 911 for the police. Weapons are lethal; no child should intentionally put him or herself in a situation were a weapon is being wielded.

During Amber's assault, the noise she created by yelling, screaming, honking the horn, and fighting back, alerted a neighbor a half a block away. This young man's name is Lee Larson. He did not know Amber and wasn't even sure of what was happening to her in the park. But instead of ignoring her cries for help, he ran toward the confronta-

56

tion. His intervention frightened the assailant, who quickly fled, leaving Amber free to run towards Lee and safety. He took her to his mother's home and called the police and Amber's father.

It makes us sick inside to think what might have happened to Amber if Lee hadn't felt the responsibility to come to her aid. His actions are commendable and inspiring! He is a modern-day hero.

"I relive it. Often. "
     -an assaulted child

9

SUMMARY

We realize that the thought of anyone hurting a child just goes against the grain for most of us. We also realize that some of the ideas or scenarios that we've described in this guide may be upsetting and uncomfortable. They upset us, too. But try to step outside of your discomfort for the sake of your children and decide to teach your children some life-saving self-defense skills, attitudes, and habits.

We believe that every parent is capable of teaching their children self-defense or self-protection skills. If you do not, you are doing your children a great disservice and putting their lives in unnecessary jeopardy.

As martial artists, of course we feel that the best way to train your children is to have them taught by an expert in a karate school situation. There really is no comparable substitute for this type of intense training. However, we realize that the majority of children will never set a foot inside a karate school in their lifetime, yet they shouldn't be denied self-defense training. They can be taught basic skills at home; Amber saved her own life without having formal self-defense training.

Unfortunately, there are drawbacks to giving children just a brief education in self-defense, especially if the child somehow gets an over-confident or invincible attitude as a result. It's vital that your children understand the purpose for learning the skills and the responsibility that goes along with having this vital knowledge.

As parents, we want more than anything for our children to be safe and sound. And now we have a way to get closer to this dream...

10

SELF-DEFENSE QUIZ

Ask your children the following questions:

1. Name three self defense tools.
   _____
   _____
   _____

2. Name three self-defense weapons.
   _____
   _____
   _____

3. Name three self-defense targets.
   _____
   _____
   _____

4. List some trusted adults.
   _____
   _____
   _____
   _____

5. What kinds of things might be said during a verbal attack?

_____

_____

_____

6. Who might hurt you?

_____

_____

_____

7. What number do you call to reach the police?

_____

8. Name three good self-defense habits.

_____

_____

_____

9. List two things you can do if you are attacked.

_____

_____

10. What could you say to a bully to make him or her go away?

_____

_____

_____

SAFE AND SOUND PRODUCTIONS PRESENTS:

WORKSHOPS ON SELF-PROTECTION FOR KIDS

Facilitated by Gordon Franks and Susan Erling,

the authors of

SAFE & SOUND

—lecture

—demonstration

—hand-outs

WHO: For parents and their kids up to age 16

WHAT: A 2-hour workshop on how to develop self-protective life-styles for parents and kids

WHY: To offer easy, practical, powerful ways in which parents can teach their children self-defensive skills, attitudes, and habits

WHEN: As requested.

WHERE: As requested.

FOR MORE INFORMATION: CALL 612-USA-1234

Karate helps kids HIT the books, BREAK bad habits and BEAT failure.

THE POWERFUL ALTERNATIVE

Call now for a FREE INTRODUCTORY LESSON.

KARATE

The *Powerful* Alternative

CALL: (612) USA-1234

KARATE MASTER
Learn Karate

International champions Pat Worley and Gordon Franks teach you the flexibility strength, and mental conditioning that is involved in karate. The basic movements for self defense as well as various kicks and strikes are demonstrated in this detailed instructional video.

$14⁹⁵
Mfg. Sugg. Retail

CALL: (612) USA-1234

MEET THE AUTHORS

GORDON FRANKS is a former world karate champion, a sixth degree black belt, a self-defense consultant for police departments, co-star of *Karate Master*, and owner of USA Karate Schools in Minneapolis.

SUSAN ERLING is the mother of an assaulted child, a brown belt karate student, a free-lance writer, and director of the Pregnancy and Infant Loss Center in Minnesota.